# Renaissance Music for Flute

## John Holenko





*WWW.MELBAY.COM*

# John Holenko

John Holenko has performed on classical guitar, steel-string guitar, mandolin, banjo and historic instruments as a soloist and chamber musician. As a member of the early music ensemble Sonus, Mr. Holenko has performed on historic instruments in recitals in the United States and in Europe and performs on mandolin and steel-string guitar with his group The Hungry Monks, an eclectic, acoustic ensemble playing a wide variety of traditional and original music.

He has been on the faculty of Charleston Southern University and The College of Charleston. He is also the guitarist/mandolinist/banjo player for the Charleston Symphony Orchestra. Mr. Holenko is very active in music education through his own private studio, Hungry Monk Music, residencies throughout the US, and most recently as an instructor with the American Music Systems.

Mel Bay Publications has published editions of Medieval music and Renaissance music for mandolin by Mr. Holenko.

His recordings include Medieval music on historic instruments, Irish music on solo guitar and mandolin, original and traditional music on guitar and mandolin, and New Age recordings on guitar and percussion.

Mr. Holenko received degrees in classical guitar performance from the New England Conservatory, and the University of Southern California, also studying historic performance at both institutions, and premiering many new works.

# Index of Tunes

# Introduction

The melodies in this book were being played in what is called the Renaissance period in music. This historical period in music is generally thought of as beginning around 1450, a more or less arbitrary date that indicates certain musical trends evident in the music of several Italian composers, and continuing into the early 1600's depending on geographic location. Musical ideas and fashion, indeed information in general, traveled much slower than we are accustomed to expect today. Many of the melodies presented here are of uncertain origin and enjoyed a long and varied life as composers, arrangers, and publishers found new ways of using these tunes as the basis for instrumental variations, dances, and songs. The melodies here come from a variety of different sources. Some are melodies from the songs that were so popular at the time. There are many dance tunes and also a few sets of chord changes to be improvised over. These sets of chords were called "grounds". Some of these melodies are taken from music published for the solo lute, while others are taken from 4 and 5 part scores intended for a variety of instruments.

Whether the tunes came from songs or instrumental settings, it is usually fairly easy to determine the proper chords underlying these melodies. Occasionally, the chords can be altered or even ignored in favor of a steady drone with the root and fifth of the key.

## Tunes

You will find many types of dances and popular tunes in this collection. The court dances of the time provided composers with the structure to construct some of the period's most enjoyable melodies. Some dance melodies may have originally had words, but have gone on to a life as instrumentals only.

## Songs

Many of these melodies are taken from popular songs of the time. The Renaissance may have been one of the most prolific songwriting periods in musical history. All the great composers of the day wrote songs and many of them were published and performed both at court and in private. No lyrics are included here. Even without the words, these are wonderful tunes.

## Grounds

There are a couple of examples of grounds. Grounds are a set of chord changes that can be used to improvise over. This is not unlike a contemporary folk, rock, or bluegrass tune whose chords are used for "jamming". Some grounds are taken from actual songs (Greensleeves), some are from dances (Folias).

## Flute Instrumentation

While musicians of the time would have played these tunes on very different instruments than we have at our disposal today, we do play the modern equivalent of many of them.

Renaissance wind instruments include the recorder, flute, crumhorn, or cornetto. This edition of the Tune Book is set for the modern flute in keys that make sense on that instrument.

The most popular accompaniment instrument during the Renaissance was the lute, and although the modern guitar is a very different instrument, it is used in much the same way as the lute. The guitar, or any other instrument with the ability to play the chords indicated in this music, would be a good choice for accompanying these melodies.

Another interesting aspect of Renaissance musical practice was the use of percussion. Modern percussion instruments such as tambourine, frame drum, bells, or any other hand percussion would be appropriate for some of the livelier of these tunes.

## Performance

You will find the tunes in this book written in their most basic forms. The melodies come from either the instrumental editions available, from the vocal line of songs, or from the melody line of lute tablatures. The melodies are suitable for the modern flute and the chords can be played on any chordal instrument.

Performers are encouraged to use these melodies as a basis for improvisation. Melodies can be ornamented by the use of trills or by filling in the notes between intervals in the melodic line. Variations on the basic melody can be performed, and in fact some of the melodies are actually written out variations. There are a couple of chord sequences given that can simply be improvised over using the given scale.

In a few cases, such as the Canarios, a chord rhythm line of music is given to indicate specific rhythmic ideas. In these melodies, the use of a rhythmic device called a hemiola is often used, usually in the context of a time signature of 6/8. The basic idea is that a group of 6 eighth notes can be grouped into either two groups of three, or three groups of two. Both of these add up to six beats and the eighth note stays the same in both. The effect is one of either 2 beats per measure or 3 beats per measure.

If the accompanist follows this rhythm scheme, the melody will be supported properly and the true intent of the music will come out.

Sometimes the rhythmic line indicates where chords change independent of the melodic line.

*Taken from a solo for the lute, Robert Johnson was one of England's premiere lute composers and teachers.*

# Alman

Robert Johnson

*This is the melody line from the polyphonic setting by Praetorious.*

# Ballet

Michael Praetorious
Terpsichore 1612

*This is the melody line from the collection called Danserye by Tielman Susato. This tune, along with all the others from this collection, is a setting of a popular dance tune of the time. Susato provided the alto, tenor, and bass parts to this tunes soprano part.*

# Bergerette: Sans Roch

Tielman Susato
Danserye 1551

# The Bishop

Miss Dolland's Delight

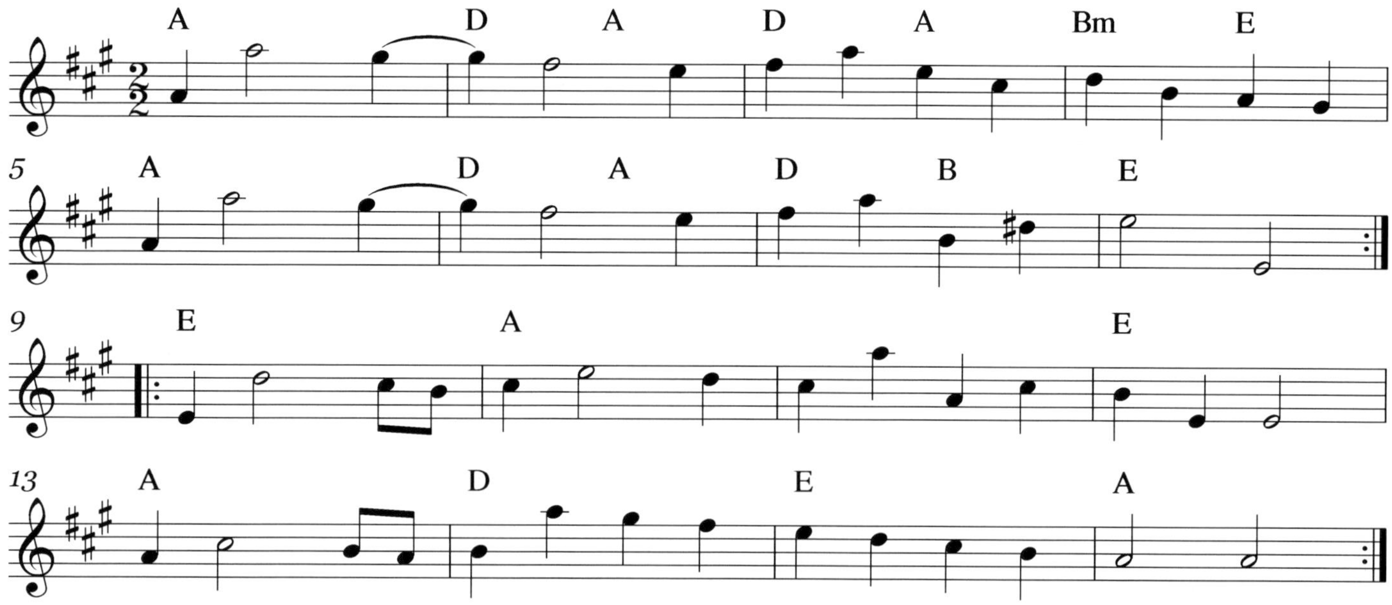


*A popular tune from the English repertoire.*

# Bonny Sweet Robin

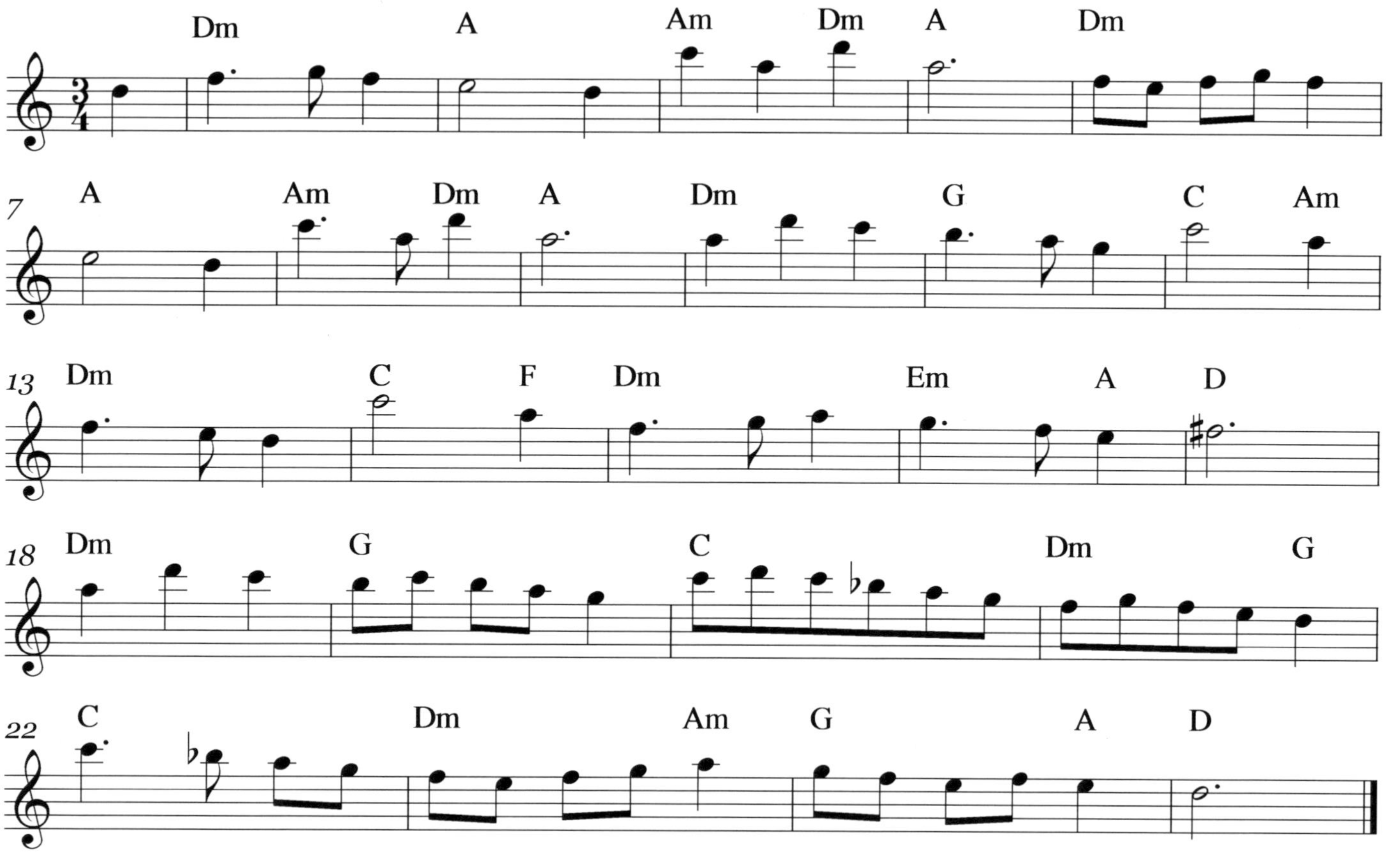

*Another of Praetorious' tunes collected for his collection of tunes entitled Terpischore.*

# Branle Double

Michael Praetorious
Terpsichore 1612

*A tune from the English country dance repertoire found in Playford's collection.*

# Childgrove

*Another tune from the English country dance repertoire.*

# Christchurch Bells

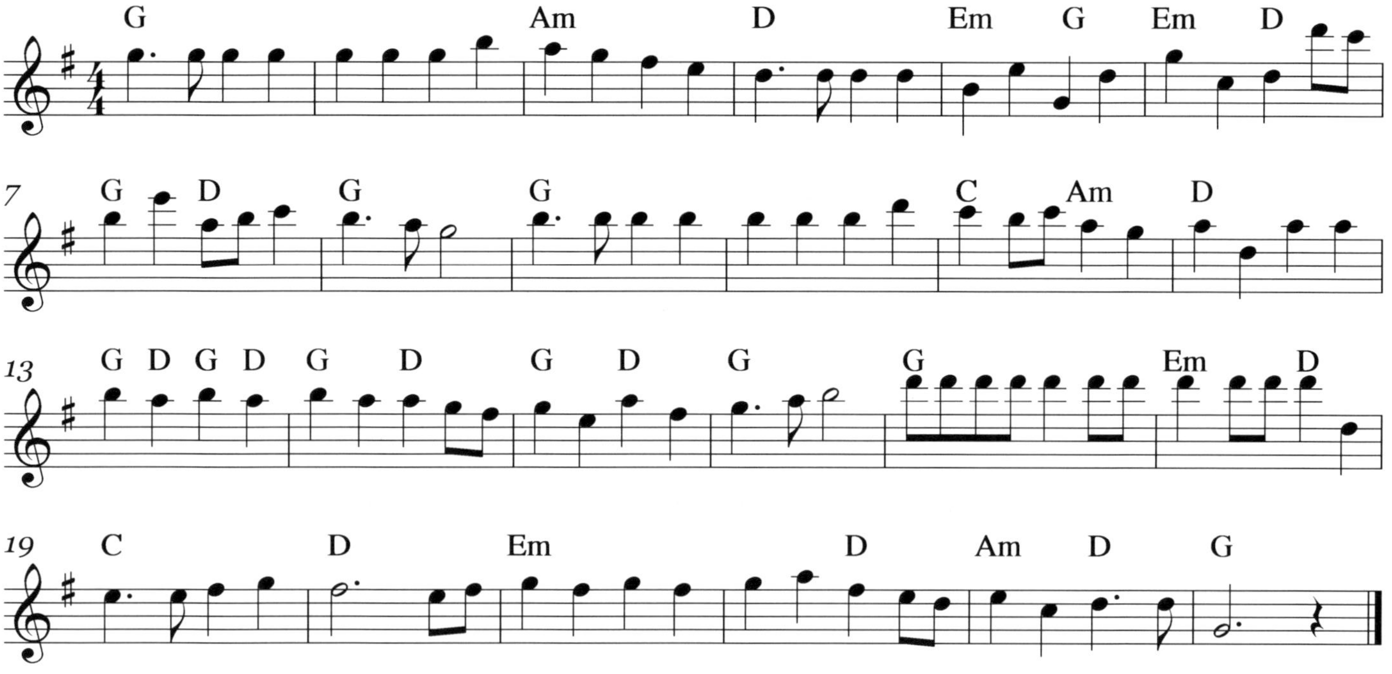

*Taken from one of the solo versions for Baroque guitar by the Spanish composer Gaspar Sanz. The Canarios was a dance supposedly representative of the Canary Islands.*

# Canarios

Based on the version by
Gaspar Sanz 1674

27
D A D A D G A D
32
G A D A E A D G A
37
D G D A D
42
A G D G A D A
47
G A G A D G D A
52
D A D A D G A D

*From a duo for 2 lutes by John Johnson, this is a good example of a set of variatins on a repeating chord progression.*

# Dump

John Johnson
d. 1594

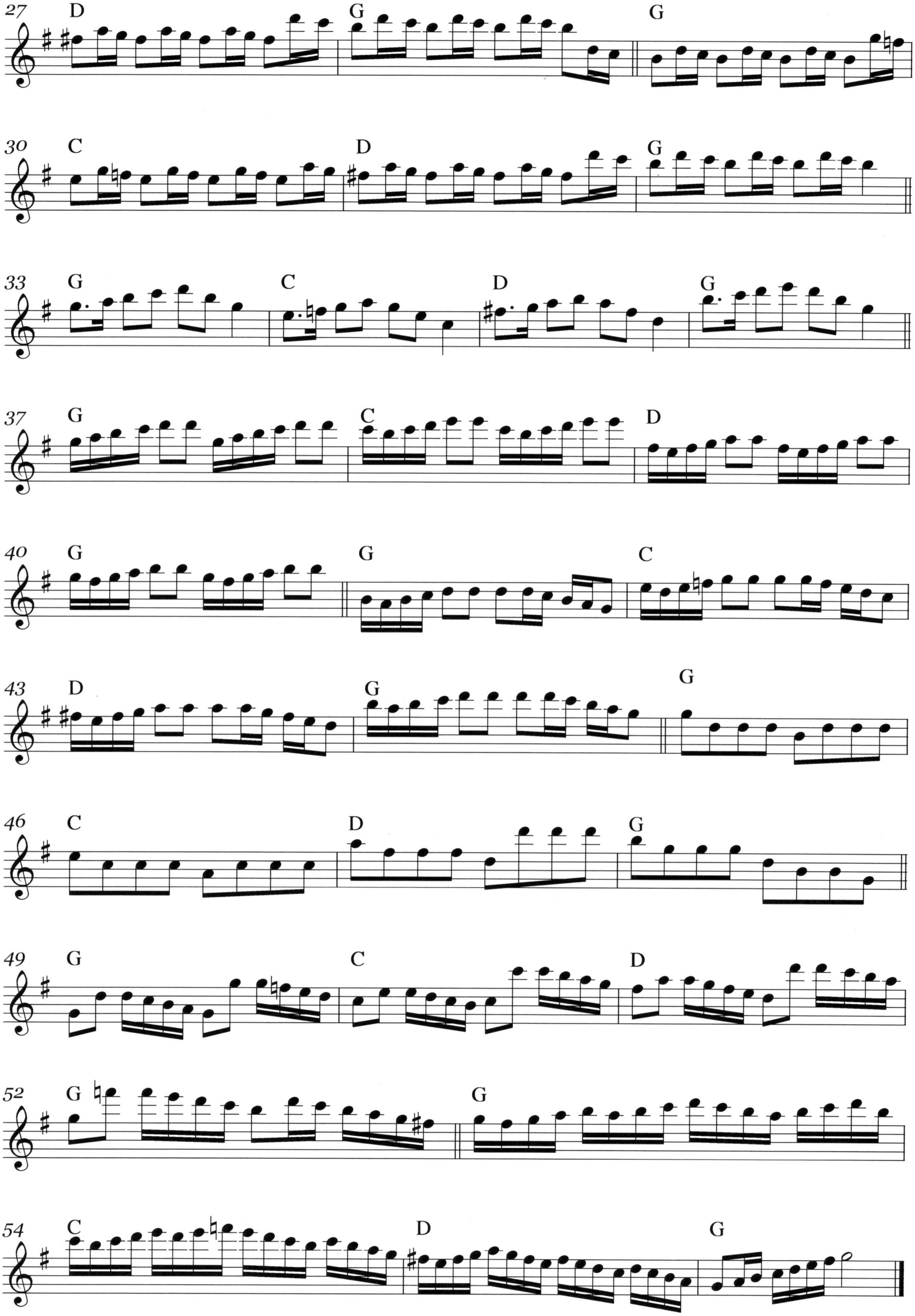
27 D G G
30 C D G
33 G C D G
37 G C D
40 G G C
43 D G G
46 C D G
49 G C D
52 G G
54 C D G

*Another of Susato's tunes. Watch the placement of the chords within the measures. The change of chord on beat 2 in some measures adds to the rhythmic interest.*

# Dont vient cela

Tielman Susato
Danserye 1551

*Literally "The Jew's Dance", this is a melody taken form the solo for lute.*

# Der Juden Tanz

Hans Newsidler

*This is a very popular English tune. Watch out for the change from 6/8 time to 3/4 time. The eighth note stays the same. If you follow the chord rhythm you will accent the beat properly.*

# The Fairie Round

*This melody comes from an Elizabethan song by John Dowland who is considered one of the finest, if not the finest, lute players and composers of the Renaissance.*

# Fine Knacks for Ladies

John Dowland
2nd Book of Airs (1600)

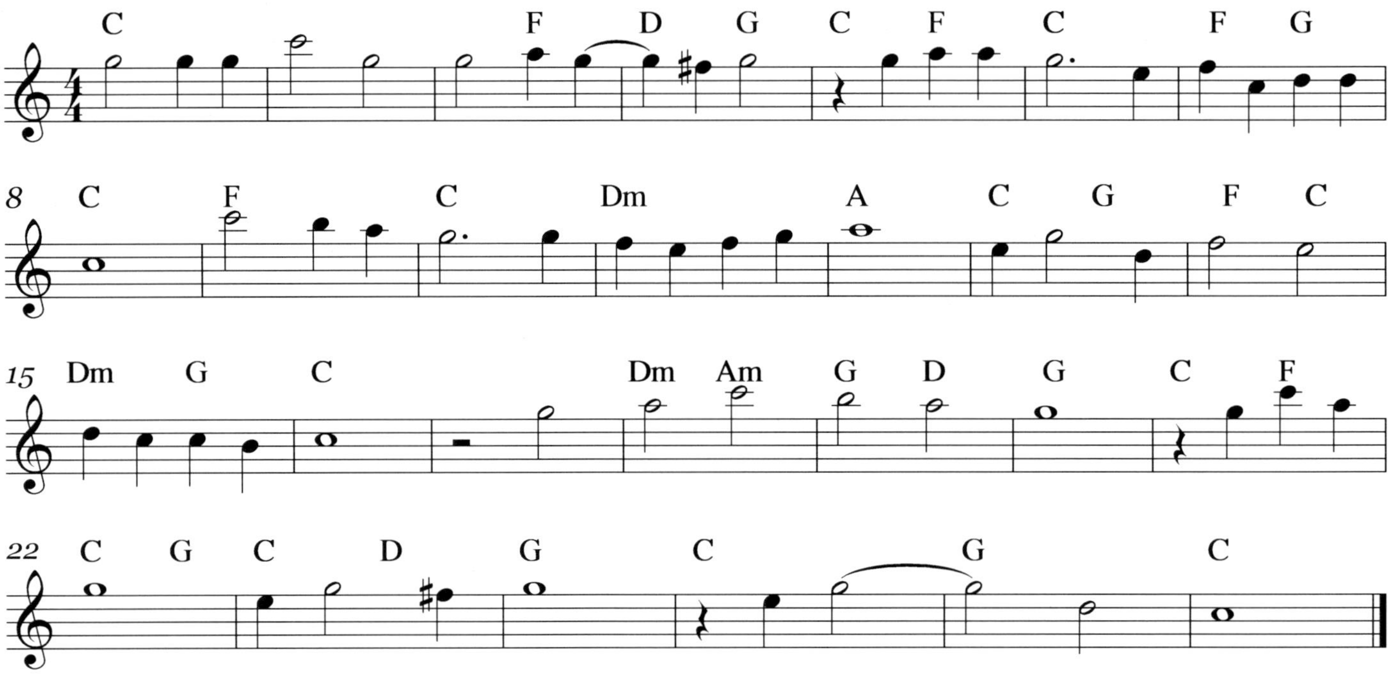


*A slow, sad song found in many instrumental and vocal arrangement.*

# Fortune My Foe

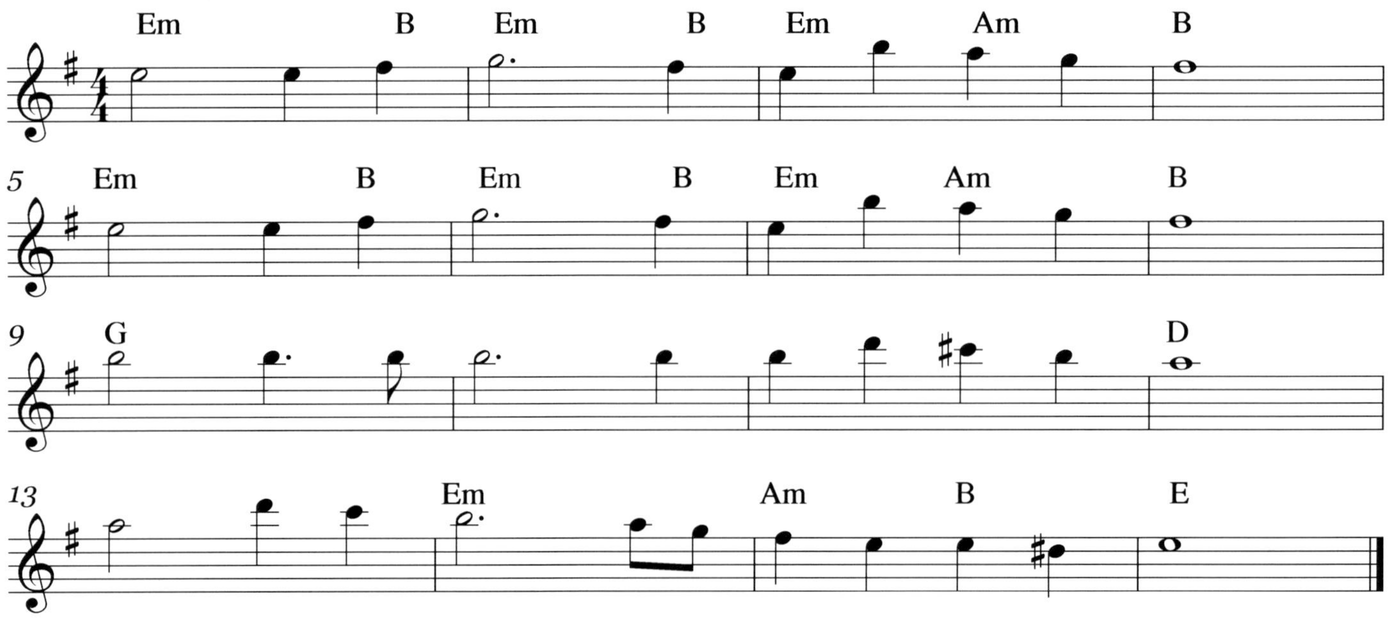

*The melody comes from a John Dowland song, "Now, oh now my needs must part." Even without words, the melodies of Dowland's songs are beautiful and memorable.*

# The Frog Galliard

John Dowland

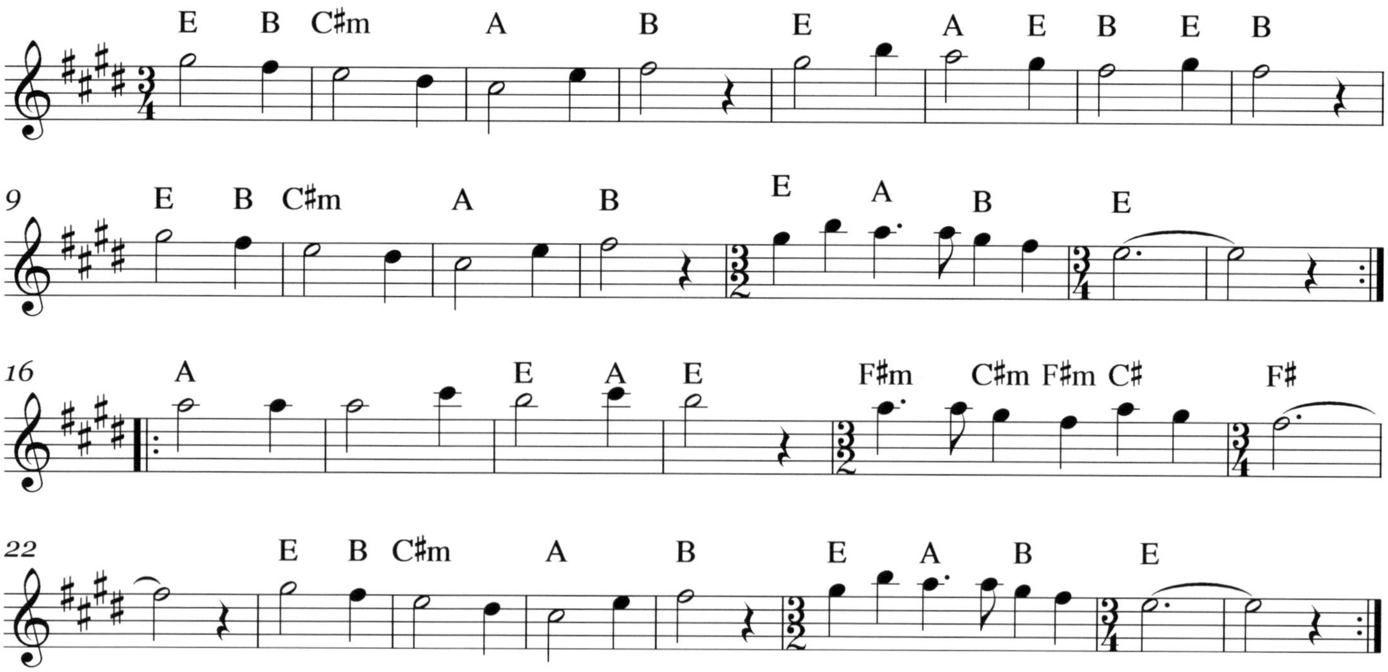

*The variation on this tune come from a setting for solo lute.*
*Several settings exist, the best known being the song.*

# Go From My Window

*This melody was taken from a solo for the Renaissance cittern, which is sort of an early mandolin.*

# Grimstock

*The melody that most people think of when they think of Renaissance music. Renaissance musicians were usually proficient improvisers and used the chord changes to "Greensleeves" as a ground with which to make new variations. The chord changes given can be varied slightly. The E chords could all be either major or minor. When improvising with the given scale, be sure to take into account whether your E is major (G sharp) or minor (G natural). You also have the option of using an F natural or an F sharp.*

# Greensleeves scale

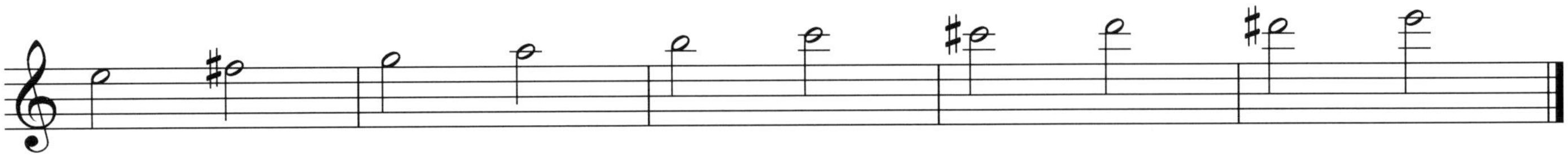

# Greensleeves

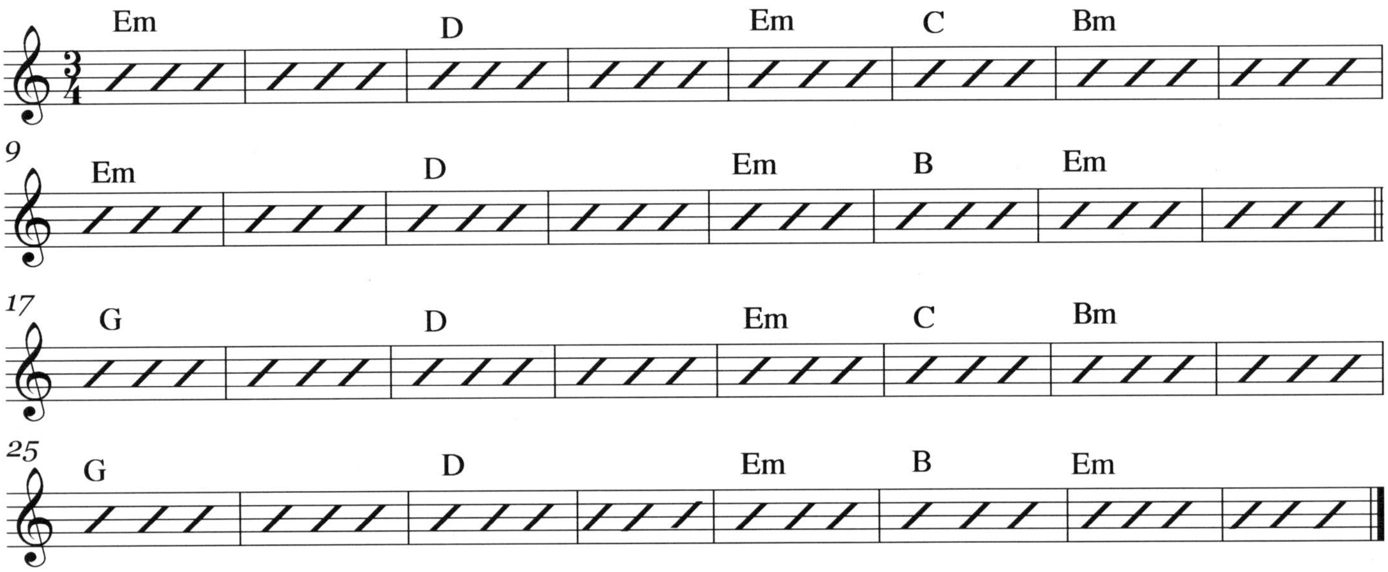

# Greensleeves

*"Guard My Cows" is a very famous solo for the Spanish vihuela, which is basically shaped like a guitar but tuned like a lute.*

# Guardeme las vacas

Luis de Narvaez
variations based on his solos for vihuela

*A somewhat bawdy English song celebrating wedded bliss.*

# Heigh Ho for a Husband

# John Come Kiss Me Now

*The melody from a multi-part setting that I have heard played by modern brass quintets.*

# The Honeysuckle

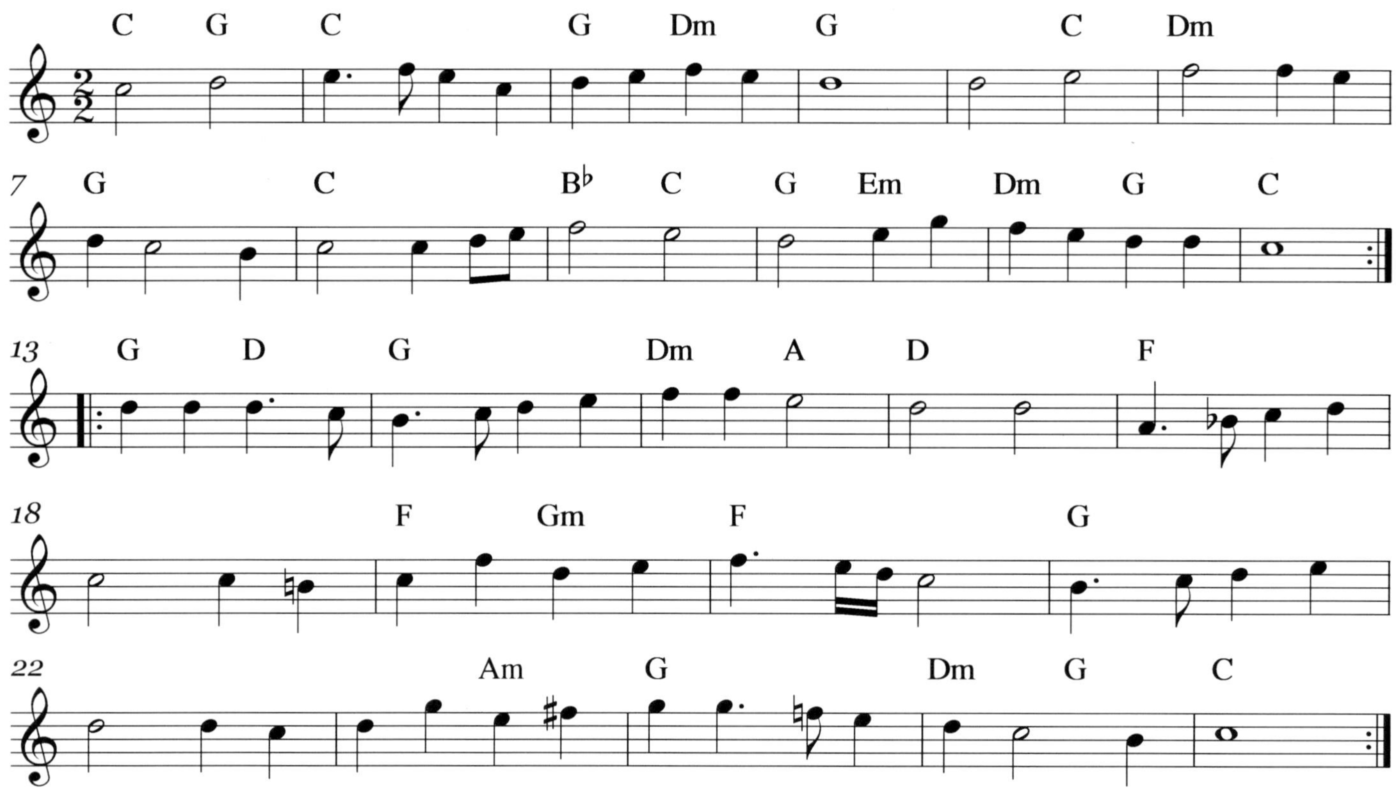


*Taken from a lute song by Thomas Campion.*

# I Care Not for These Ladies

Thomas Campion

*A very short tune with words typical of the good-time party tune so common in Elizabethan times.*

# Hey Robin, Jolly Robin

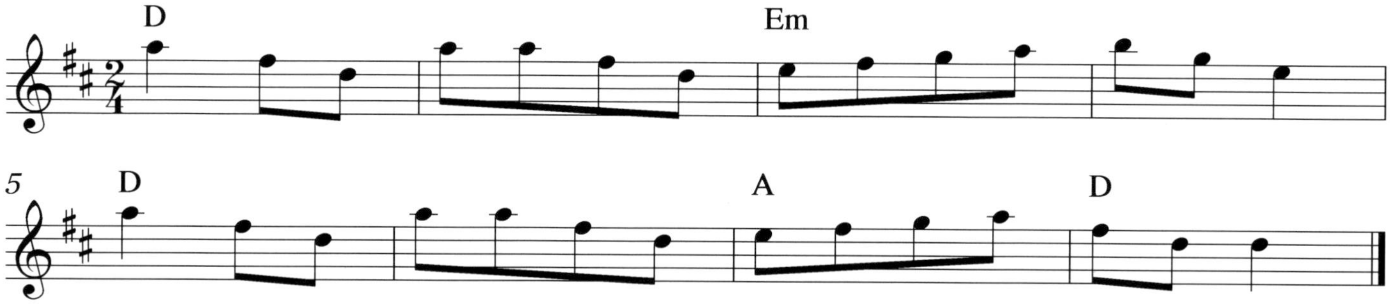


# The Hunt Is Up

*The melody is from a multi-part setting from Susato's publication.*

# Il Estoit Une Fillette

Tielman Susato
Danserye 1551

*A song composed by Thomas Morley.*

# It Was a Lover and His Lass

Thomas Morley

*A melody by the French composer of chansons.*

# J'ay Tant Bon Credit

Jacques Arcadelt

*This melody is found in a number of settings. It is not in traditional jig time, which would be 6/8.*

# Kemp's Jug

# La Bourée

Michael Praetorious
Terpsichore 1612

*There have been many settings and arrangements of the famous "La Folias" melody/chord progression. This melody comes from the Baroque guitar version by Sanz. The recurring chord progression is ideally suited to improvised variations. Pay attention to the C natural (during the C chord) and the C sharp (during the A chord).*

# La Folias de Espana

# La Folias de Espana

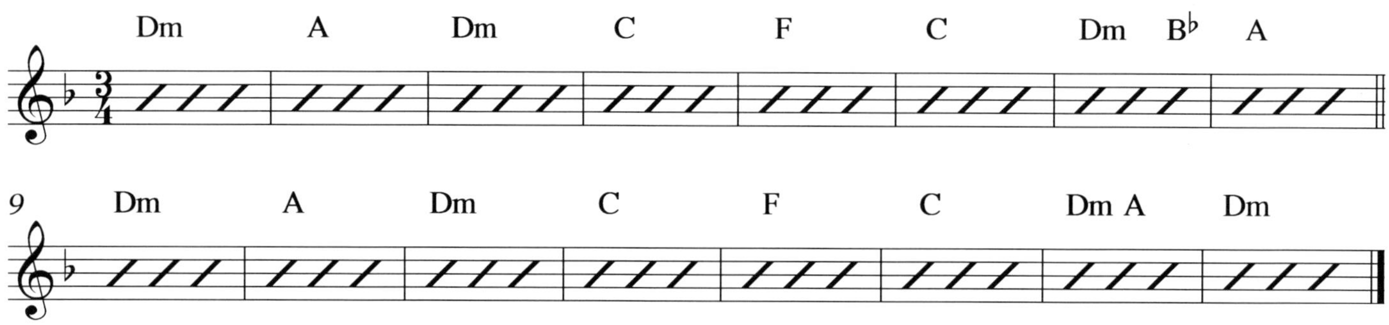

# La Folias de Espana

variations after
Gaspar Sanz 1674

*The melody is from the solo for lute.*

# Lady Hudson's Puff

John Dowland

*A beautiful melody from Tobias Hume who was known for his consort arrangements and music for the solo gamba.*

# Life

Tobias Hume

# Light 'O Love

# Lillibulero

*A bawdy drinking song in which the main character gets increasingly drunk and hallucinates.*

# Martin Said to His Man

# Mignonne allons voir si la rose

# Monsieur's Almain

# Never Weather Beaten Sail

Thomas Campion

# Now, Oh Now

John Dowland
2nd Book of Airs (1600)

*From the music of the Spanish Composer, this is a good example of a set of varitations on a recurring chord progression.*

# Passamezzo

Diego Ortiz

# Packington's Pound

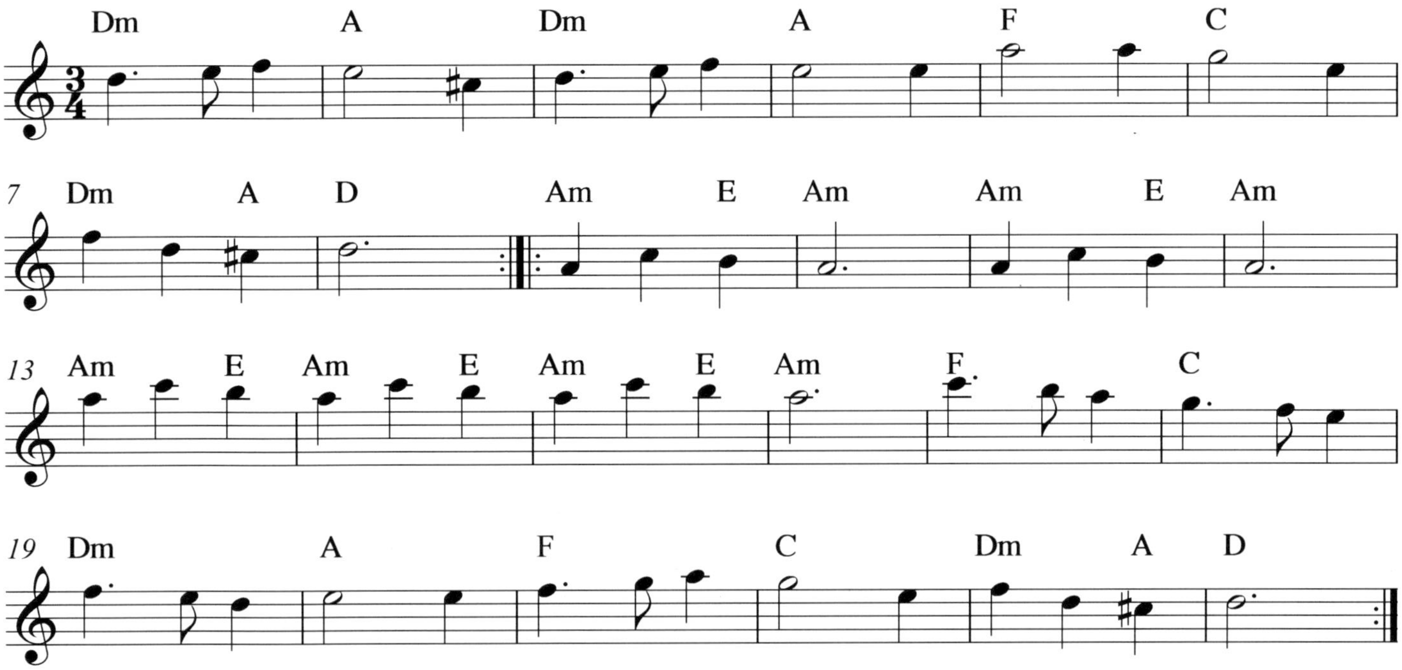


*There is some speculation that this song was composed by Henry VIII.*

# Pastime With Good Company

# Pour mon Coeur

*An old French melody from even earlier than the Renaissance.*

# Quant je voi yver

*Another melody from the multi-part setting by Praetorious. Played at a good, brisk tempo with a certain feel, this can sound like an Appalachian fiddle tune!*

# Philou

Michael Praetorious
Terpsichore 1612

# Ronde I: Por quoy

Tielman Susato
Danserye 1551

# Ronde

Tielman Susato
Danserye 1551

# Sellenger's Round

# Shepard's Dance

*This page has been left blank to avoid an awkward page turn.*

*There are many pieces with this title. This tune comes from one of the more melodic versions found in Praetorious' collection. Once again, the chord progression lends itself to improvisation. Pay attention to the C natural and C sharp, and the G natural and G sharp.*

# Spagnoletta

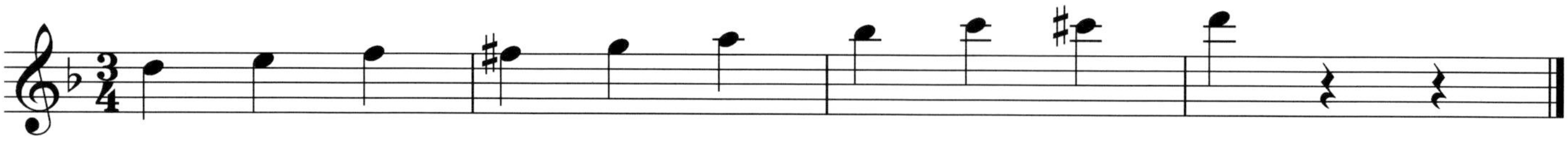

# Spagnoletta

Michael Praetorious
Terpsichore 1612

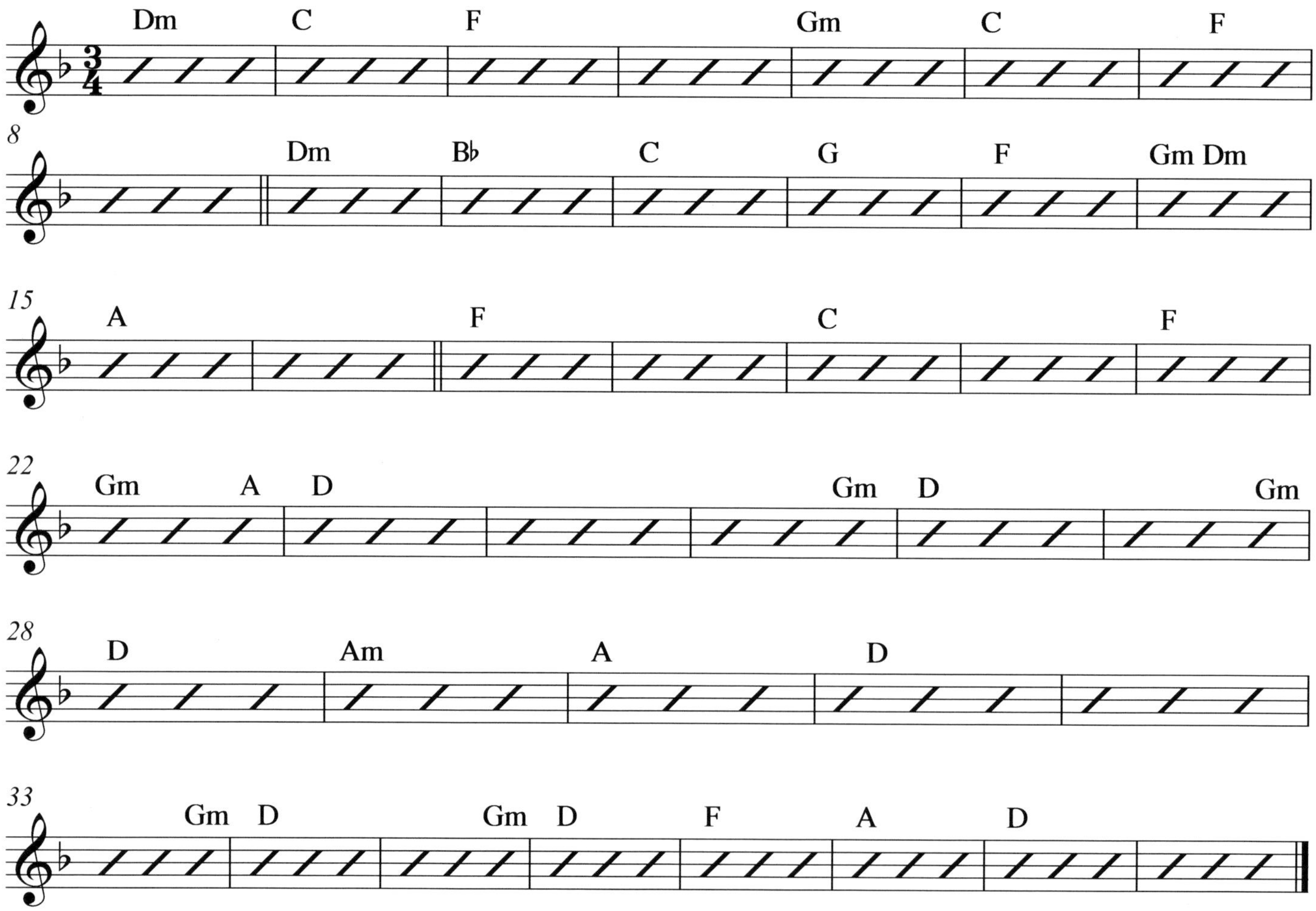

# Spagnoletta

Michael Praetorious
Terpsichore 1612

# Tant que vivray

Claudin de Sermisy
Pierre Attaignant

*This melody taken from the setting for broken consort by Thomas Morley.*

# Tarleton's Jig

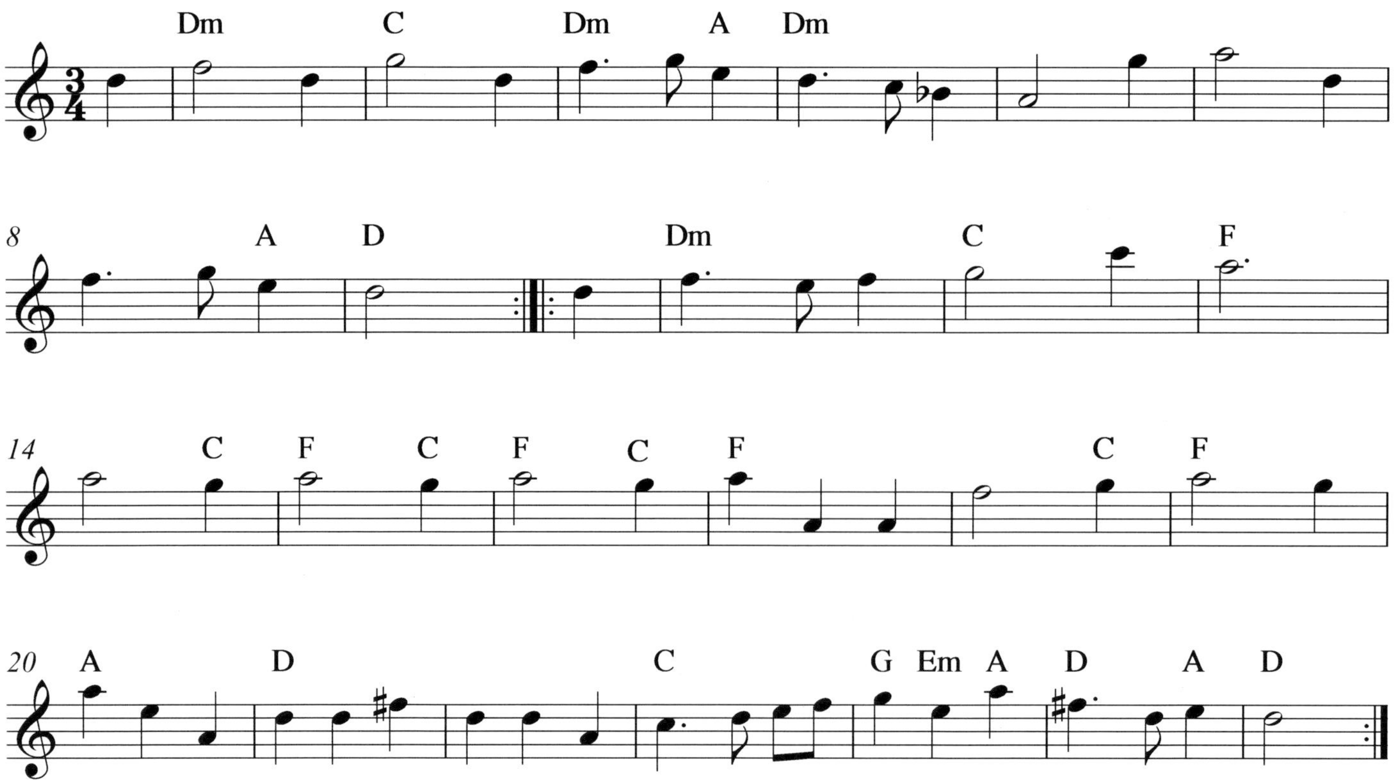

*The melody to a very lovely song. Don't let the 3/2 measure fool you.*
*Keep the quarter note the same.*

# Three Ravens

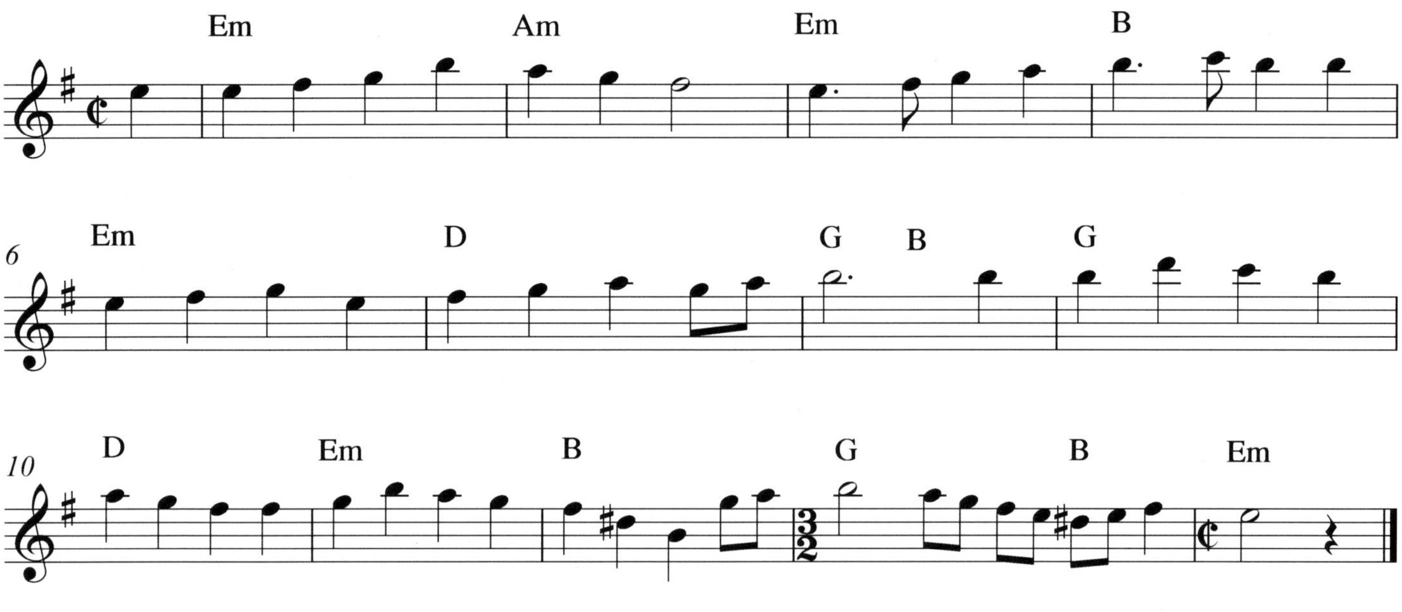


*You can feel this in 1 beat per measure. Try it with a G-D drone throughout.*

# Volte

Michael Praetorious
Terpsichore 1612

*A very bawdy song in which a young man promises to give a young lady this mysterious "Watkins Ale".*

# Watkin's Ale

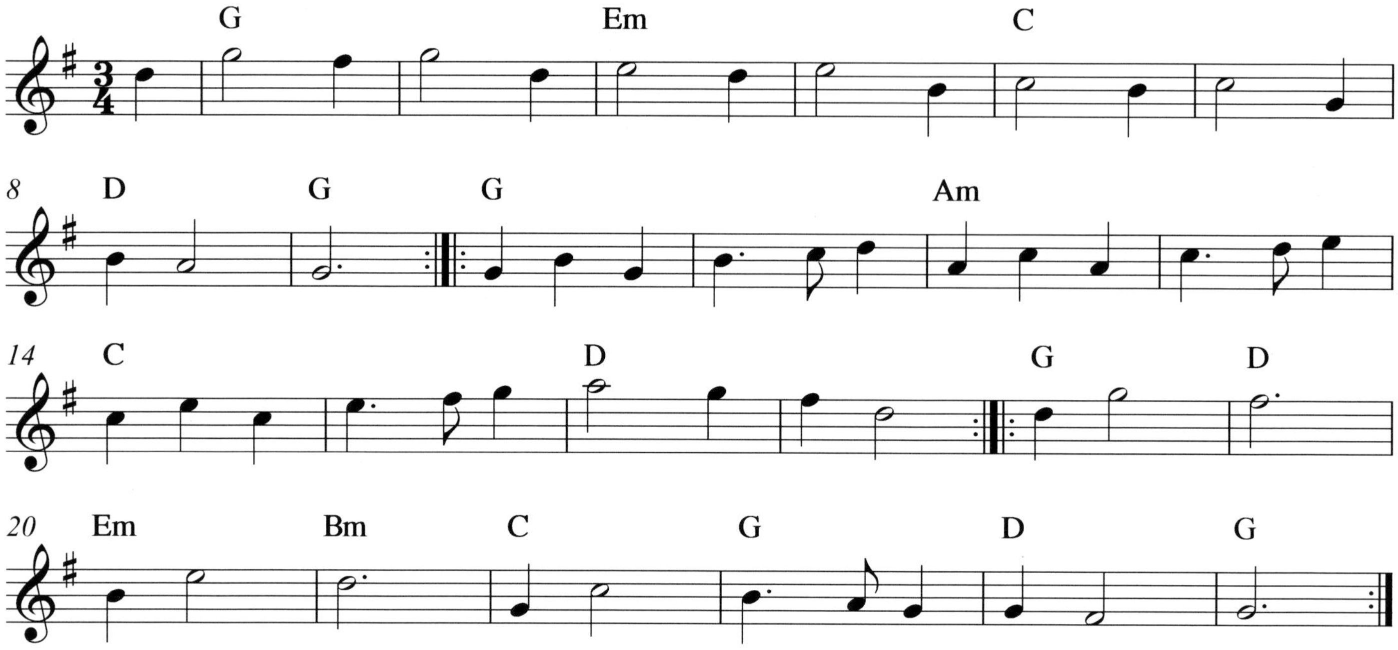


*This melody is found in several different settings. This version comes from the solo for lute.*

# Wilson's Wilde

# What if a Day

Thomas Campion

# The Willow Song

*This is basically a set of variations on a recurring chord progression.*

# Woodycock

33 Gm Dm Gm D
37 Dm C Dm D G
41 Gm Dm Gm D
45 Dm C Dm D G
49 Gm Dm Gm D
53 Gm F Dm Gm Dm D
57 F C Dm D G

# Other Mel Bay Flute Books

Down the Back Lane: Variation in Traditional Irish Dance Music (Larsen)

Essential Guide to the Irish Flute and Tin Whistle (Larsen)

150 Gems of Irish Music for Flute (Larsen)

Complete Irish Flute Book (McCaskill/Gilliam)

Complete Jazz Flute Book (W. Bay)

Essential Jazz Lines in the Style of Charlie Parker: Flute Edition (C. Christiansen)

Essential Jazz Lines in the Style of John Coltrane: Flute Edition (C. Christiansen/Bock)

Jazz Flute (Kaplan)

A Guide to Non-Jazz Improvisation: Flute Edition (Fox/Weissman)

Flute Fingering Chart (W. Bay)

Flute Handbook (McCaskill/Gilliam)

Flute Improvisation Made Easy (McCaskill/Gilliam)

100 Christmas Carols and Hymns for Flute and Guitar (W. Bay)

100 Gospel Songs and Hymns for Flute and Guitar (W. Bay)

100 Hymns for Flute and Guitar (W. Bay)

A Celtic Flute Christmas (Tanguay)

Christmas Carols for Flute & Guitar (Gendron)

Complete Book of Wedding Music for Flute or Violin (Mickelson)

Favorite Carols for Flute Solo with Piano Accompaniment (Hollins)

Gospel Flute (Mickelson)

Hymns for Flute and Piano Made Easy (McCaskill/Gilliam)

Instrumental Caroling Book (W. Bay)

My Very Best Christmas: Flute & Oboe Edition (Khanagov)

Noels for Flute and PIano (McCaskill/Gilliam)

Old English Hymns for Flute Solo (Cummings)

Playing Outside the Lines (Harrison)

Sacred Classics for Flute and Piano Made Easy (McCaskill/Gilliam)

Sacred Solos for the Flute Volume 1 (McCaskill/Gilliam)

Sacred Solos for the Flute Volume 2 (McCaskill/Gilliam)

Wedding Music for Flute & Guitar (Gendron)